typing for beginners

by

betty owen

illustrations by patricia malkin

GROSSET & DUNLAP
A Filmways Company
PUBLISHERS   NEW YORK

Printed in the United States of America

table of contents

Other Things You Should Know

the preliminaries

Why Learn to Type

How do we communicate? With words, spoken and written. And what way of getting words down on paper is faster than with a typewriter? In an office, typing is a necessity, whether it is used for correspondence or for putting information into a computer. In schools and colleges, reports and papers certainly have a more professional look when typed. And personal letters are an even greater joy to receive when they are typed and easily readable!

Typing gives you the freedom to express yourself, the freedom to go anywhere in the world and be able to get a job. Typing gives you the sense of freedom that comes from being able to do something yourself. You, too, will be typing at the end of this book.

How to Use This Book

1. Write in longhand all the reasons you *should* learn to type. Then write why you *want* to learn to type. Your success in learning will depend largely on how important typing is to you.

2. Every day before typing, review your reasons to learn and then set a goal for that day. The objectives stated at the beginning of each step will help you with this. Remember, be reasonable with your goals. An increase in speed of one word a day is excellent; a reduction of errors by one or two a day is fine. Goals which you can achieve will help you succeed.

3. Practice every day. Fifteen minutes a day is better than two hours once a week. Also, set a time each day for your practice. Early in the day when you are fresh is better than late at night when your body may be tired and it may be difficult to concentrate. To achieve the best results, set aside a definite practice time each day.

4. Typing is a *skill,* and it should not be intellectualized. Sure, you can sit down and memorize the keyboard. Your head will know where the keys are, but your fingers need many hours of practice to learn the keys. The best way to learn is to concentrate and practice regularly and often.

5. Set aside a special place for your typewriter and paper. Leave the typewriter ready for use, and you will find that you are much more likely to sit down and practice regularly, and during spare moments.

6. The top of the typewriter table should be 26 inches from the floor. If your table is higher than this, compensate for it by using a higher chair.

7. *Concentrate* on each and every letter. You'll find it necessary to slow your reading down to your typing speed. To do this, and to focus your mind on the letter you are typing, say each letter *aloud* before typing it.

Enjoy Your Typing

Sure, learning to type is hard work and may be tedious at times. We've tried to make the material in *Typing for Beginners* as interesting as possible. When you are practicing on other material, pick something you would like to read. Then, read it over before typing it so you won't be distracted by the content when you should be concentrating on each letter.

The better your typing becomes, the easier it will be. Each success will make the next step easier, and each step will give you a greater sense of accomplishment.

If you feel you must glance at the keyboard once in a while to see if your fingers are on the right keys, that is okay. But only glance. To get any degree of speed and accuracy in your typing, you must keep your eyes on your *copy*. If you are unsure about your typing, you might try looking at what you have typed rather than at the keys.

A blank keyboard? Yes, if you want to you can cover your keys with signal dots, which can be purchased at an office supply store. However, extensive research has failed to show that covered or uncovered keys make any difference in learning to type. Whichever way is the easiest for you is the best.

Good luck with your typing and enjoy your accomplishments!

Get to Know Your Typewriter

Try the various levers and buttons on your typewriter so that you'll know what they are about. The booklet which came with your machine will give you specific information.

The essential parts of a typewriter are shown on the two drawings of electric and manual machines and are listed below. Find each part on your typewriter.

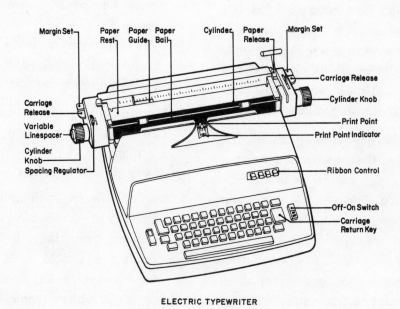

ELECTRIC TYPEWRITER

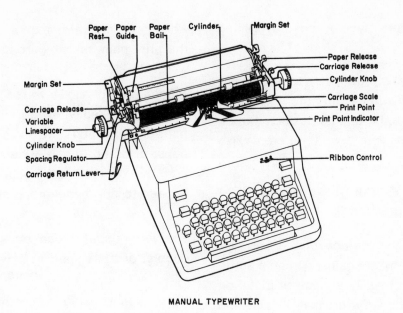

Paper Rest · Paper Guide · Paper Bail · Cylinder · Margin Set · Paper Release · Carriage Release · Cylinder Knob · Carriage Scale · Print Point · Print Point Indicator · Margin Set · Carriage Release · Variable Linespacer · Cylinder Knob · Spacing Regulator · Carriage Return Lever · Ribbon Control

MANUAL TYPEWRITER

Carriage release can be depressed so you can move the carriage from side to side. There is usually a carriage release on both the right and left sides of a typewriter.

Carriage return key on electric typewriters sends the carriage to the left margin so you are ready to type the next line. The paper moves up one, two, or three lines as set by the spacing regulator.

Carriage return lever on manual typewriters is used to return the carriage to the left margin so that the next line can be typed. The paper moves up one, two, or three lines depending on how the spacing regulator is set.

Carriage scale shows the spaces on each line. The scale can appear in front of the roller or on the paper rest.

Cylinder or *roller* is hard rubber and holds the paper in position for typing. It is sometimes called the *platen.*

Cylinder knob turns the cylinder or roller which moves the paper up and down.

Margin set on the left controls the left-hand margin and the one on the right controls the right-hand margin. A margin is the space between the typing and the edge of the paper.

Some machines have margins which are set by depressing the lever and moving the carriage to the position of the desired margin. On some typewriters, you just move the margin stop on the front scale to the correct position. On the IBM standard and "Executive," it is necessary to depress the carriage return key first and then to hold down the margin *Reset* key and move the carriage to the desired margin before releasing the reset key. Experiment with your machine.

Off—on switch on electric typewriters is usually on the right-hand side on the keyboard. On some typewriters, it is *under* the keyboard on the right side.

Paper bail is a metal bar with rubber rollers to hold the paper flat against the roller. This makes for quieter typing and the printing looks better.

Paper guide shows you where to put the paper in the typewriter each time. The guide slides left and right, and its position can be changed when you use a different size paper.

Paper release can be depressed to straighten the paper in the typewriter.

Paper rest is the surface of the carriage which the paper lies against. On an electric typewriter, it is usually a piece of metal on top of the roller. On a manual, it is behind the roller.

Print point shows where the typewriter key will strike the paper.

Print point indicator marks the position of the print point on the carriage scale.

Ribbon control allows you to type on the top part of the inked typewriter ribbon, or on the bottom half which may be red on some ribbons, or on no ribbon. When set for no ribbon, the keys strike the paper directly. This is used to cut mimeograph stencils.

Spacing regulator can be set for single, double, or triple spacing between lines.

Variable linespacer frees the paper from single, double, or triple spacing as set by the spacing regulator. Push in the left-hand cylinder knob and you will be able to roll the paper to any place up and down the page.

Get Ready to Type

1. Your typewriter should be 26 inches from the floor. If your table is higher, use a higher chair.

2. Your typewriter should be squarely in front of you. The base of it should be approximately 9 or 10 inches from your stomach.

3. Your book can be on either the right or left side of the typewriter. Tilt your book for easier reading.

4. Check your paper guide. It should be either at 0 or in a position so that the center of your paper is at the center mark on your typewriter. On IBM typewriters the position for the paper guide for 8½″ X 11″ sheets is marked with a small horizontal line on the paper rest.

Put the left edge of your paper against the paper guide each time you insert the paper in your machine. This way your margins will always be the same.

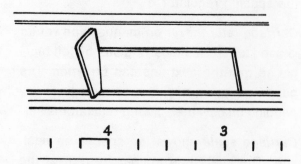

5. Roll the paper into the typewriter.

6. Straighten your paper in the typewriter. Use the paper release to loosen the paper. Bring the top edge of the paper up to meet the bottom edge and your paper will be straight.

8

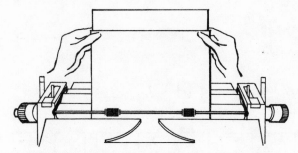

7. Reset the paper bail so that it holds the paper firmly against the cylinder. Move the rolls on the paper bail to edge of each side of the paper.

8. Roll your paper into typing position by turning the cylinder knobs. The top edge of your paper should be held by the rolls on the paper bail.

9. Set your line space regulator at either single or double space. Material which is double spaced is easier to read. However, you can save paper on your practice work by single spacing it.

10. Set 1-inch margins on the left and right side of your typewriter according to the instructions with your typewriter. If you have the larger size type, called *pica,* you will have 65 spaces across the page, with 1-inch margins. Pica type has 10 letters and spaces per inch. If you have the smaller type, called *elite,* you will have a 78-space line. Elite type has 12 letters and spaces per inch.

Pica type: 10 letters to 1 inch

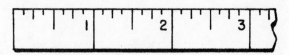

Elite type: 12 letters to 1 inch

11. Check your body position:
    a. Back straight.
    b. Feet flat on floor a few inches apart.
    c. Dangle your arms at your side. Raise your hands and place them on the keyboard without moving your elbows. You should not have to reach for the typewriter.

12. Place your hands on the home keys: Left hand on A S D F. Right hand on J K L ; .
    a. On an electric typewriter, your fingers will be slightly curved as shown in the picture. Hold your fingers as close to the keys as possible without touching them.

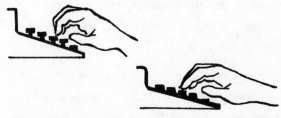

    b. On a manual, curve your fingers more, as if they were over a ball. Rest them lightly on the home row keys.

You are now ready for Step 1.

Step 1

Objective: To learn home-row keys **a s d f j k l ;**

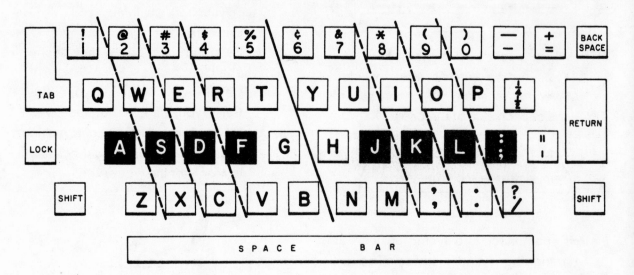

POSITION CHECK: Feet flat on floor. Typewriter squarely in front of you, one handspan from waist to typewriter.

Dangle your arms down at your sides. Pick up your hands and place them on the typewriter. Starting with the left hand, place your little finger on the "A" key, then your ring finger on "S," middle finger on "D," and index finger on "F."

Then, with the right hand, place your little finger on the semicolon, then your ring finger on "L," middle finger on "K," and index finger on "J."

These are your home-row keys. *Your fingers should return to their home after striking each key.* The fingers not being used stay at home.

On a manual typewriter, strike the key with a nice sharp stroke—not a hard stroke, but a *fast* one. The sound should be sharp and

quick. If you are pushing your keys rather than striking them, the sound will be mushy.

Strike the "J" key 3 times. Now look at your paper. Are your letters sharp? Or do they have a shadow? If they have a shadow or are printing double, you are probably pushing the keys too hard. Strike the "J" key very slightly with a sharp blow. See the difference?

Let's start using the space bar. That's the big bar in the front of the typewriter. Strike the space bar with your right thumb—*always your right thumb.* Tuck your left thumb under the palm of your hand; you won't be using it for anything in typing.

The secret of typing is concentration and keeping your mind on each letter. To do this, it is important to *say each letter aloud before you type it.* Keep your eyes on the book and say each letter. Glance at the *picture* of the keyboard to determine which finger to use. Your accuracy is much greater when you look at the text. If you feel you must check yourself, look at the paper to see what you've typed. Now, type this line of home-row letters, using the fingers shown on the chart:

```
jjj fff jjj kkk fff ddd jkl jkl jkl
```

At the end of the line, throw your carriage if you have a manual or use the carriage return key if you have an electric.

On a manual, use the index finger of your left hand to sweep the carriage return lever on the left all the way to the right. Be sure the carriage goes all the way to the left margin.

On an electric typewriter, use the little finger of your right hand to push the carriage return key. Keep all your other fingers on their home-row keys. Try it.

Let's try more typing. Position check first: Feet flat on floor, sit up straight, fingers on home-row keys. Say each letter aloud before typing it.

```
jjj fff jjj kkk fff ddd jkl jkl jkl

jjj fff jjj kkk fff ddd jkl jkl jkl

aaa ;;; lll sss kkk ddd jjj fff

aaa ;;; lll sss kkk ddd jjj fff

aaa sss as as ass ass sass

aaa sss as as ass ass sass

fff jjj kkk ddd lll sss ;;; aaa

fff jjj kkk ddd lll sss ;;; aaa
```

Look at your work. Are there any extra spaces between letters? This happens on a manual typewriter if you are pushing your keys and holding them down too long. Try using a faster motion with less pressure.

Type this line 3 times, saying each letter before typing it for a smooth, even pace:

```
jjkkll;; ffddssaa; all sad lads ask dad;
```

Compare your last 3 lines with the book and circle any errors you've made. Do you have 10 or fewer errors? If so, you are ready to go on to Step 2. If you have more than 10 errors, try Step 1 over again. Take a short break, however, before continuing.

Step 2

Objective: To learn new keys **r v u m e c o .**

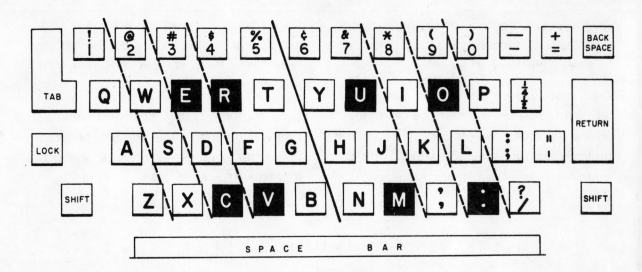

POSITION CHECK: Feet flat on floor. Typewriter squarely in front of you, one handspan away from waist. Fingers on home-row keys. Wrists up so you can balance a quarter or a nickel on the back of your hands.

Did your little fingers hurt in Step 1? They probably did because you were using muscles you normally don't use. Try holding your wrists up a little higher to relax your finger muscles and make typing easier.

Place your fingers on the home-row keys. From this position you will reach the other keys, keeping as many fingers as possible anchored on home row. Your fingers should return home after striking each letter.

Keep your eyes on the textbook. Refer to the keyboard chart for correct fingering. Type each of these lines *2 times* and say each letter before you type it:

REVIEW:	asdf jkl; asdf jkl;
NEW KEYS:	
R	frf frf rfrf rfrf drd drd krk krk drd frf
	ral rak fra fral kras sar jar jars lard
V	frfvf frfvf fvf fvf vfvf vfvf jav lav fav
	fav favrs kav vkr sav vak a;fv fvf afvf

```
U     ;lkjuj juj juj uju uju dus usj sud fuj;

      jus jud suj dull lull sul full rul urv;


M     ;lkjujmj jmj mjmj mal mad mul jams mak;

      mak lam vamus famus sam mam dam maj ram


E     asded ded eded led lead less jells sells

      kemed medkle feels meals real reels veal


C     asdedcd dcd cdcd edcd cuss cull ecc sack

      ducks crum creak creek calls jackle jackass


O     ;lol lol olol loff old soar sofa loaf aloof

      roll role cold doors roof rooves sold fold
```

Note: Between every sentence there are 2 spaces. Practice this by putting 2 spaces after each period below.

```
      ;lol. a. s. d. f. j. k. l. . .....
```

You now know 16 keys—over half of the alphabet. You'll be using these keys over and over, and you will keep correcting yourself as you go. At this stage, you should concentrate on hitting the keys with a sharp bulletlike stroke. Type the following paragraph 3 times, typing a little faster each time. Say every letter before you type it.

```
      sue cares for kev.  kev cares for sue.  jack flees dad.  red

      leaves fall free.  red mums are real.  cold ducks creak.

      real leaves soar over us.  sara feels free as a duck.  sam loves

      red; mom loves mauve.
```

There are 200 strokes in the above copy. If you had 10 errors, you were 95 percent accurate. If you had 20 errors, you were 90 percent accurate. You are ready to go on to Step 3, but take a short break before typing any more.

Step 3

Objective: To learn new letters i , w x q z p /

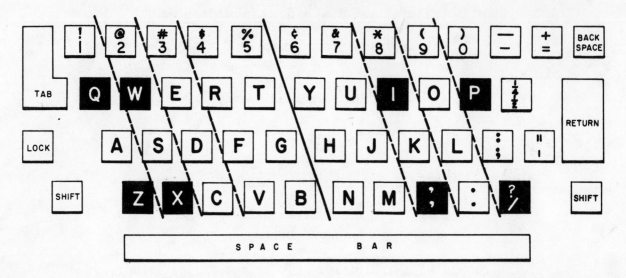

POSITION CHECK: Feet flat on floor, typewriter squarely in front of you. Fingers on home-row keys, wrists up.

REMINDER: Say each letter before typing it. Strike each key with a sharp, quick blow. Return your finger to home position.

REVIEW: Type this line 3 times:

```
asdf;lkj frfvf jujmj dedcd lol.1 asdfrfvf ;lkjujmj
```

NEW KEYS: Refer to keyboard picture for correct fingering. Type each line 3 times.

I   `;lkikik iii kkk sills fickle sickle side kicks`

       `kik like dike file circle rise miss vise jill.`

,   `;lkik,k k,k ,k,k a, s, d, f, r, v, c, e, l, m,`

W   `asws sws wsws iws wow slow were we were will wise`

       `aware jaws laws walk wore was wisher swear woof`

X   `asxs sxs xsxs six lax exac sox ax axex ox ix ux`

       `lxkxjxs oxs ixs uxs dexs axs sxs dxs fxs sex rex rsxs`

```
Q    aqa qaqa aqa quick quakes queer quorum aq eq oq quill

     iq uqu quacks quirk quid quad quail qualm equal

Z    aqaza aza zaza jazz quiz lizzard zip zipper zero

     zoom zool. uz iz oz ez az wiz wizard wizen of.

P    ;p; p;p ;ap pep pear pipes lip deep seep cap;

     pups sap jap rap up wipe quipe peppers pad lap

/    p;p/; ;/; /;/; a/s/d/f/e/r/v/c/x/z/q/w/p/o/k/l/j/
```

You have learned 20 letters and 3 punctuation marks—only 6 letters to go. As a review, type the following sentences as quickly as you can move your fingers:

```
sue cares for kev.  kev cares for sue.  jack flees dad.  red

leaves fall free.  red mums are real.  cold ducks creak.  real

leaves soar over us.  sara feels free as a duck.  sam loves red;

mom loves mauve.
```

Type the next sentences 3 times, trying to go faster each time:

```
will likes summer.  liza likes fall.  susie desires cold air.  sid

desires medium warm air.  does sid like susie or liza; does liza

like will or sid; does susie like all people.  jack wears a wool

scarf like zeke wears.  zeke wears red socks like jack wears.

aqua is a cool color.  are wizards quacks.
```

You are now ready for Step 4. You should take a break, however, before you continue any more typing at this time. It's a good idea to rest before you get too tired to concentrate.

Step 4

Objective: To learn new letters **g t b h y n** and capital letters.

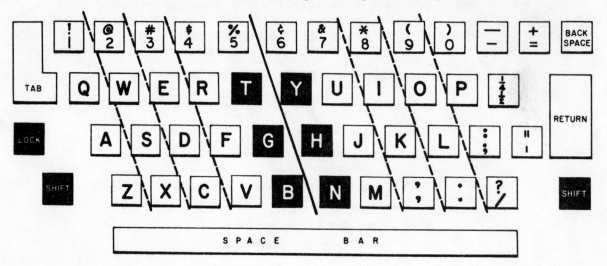

POSITION CHECK: Feet flat on floor. Fingers on home-row keys.

REMINDER: Say each letter before striking it. Return fingers to home position.

REVIEW: Type this line 3 times:

```
a;sldkfj frfv dedc swsxs aqaza kik, jujm lol.1 ;p;/;
```

NEW KEYS: Refer to keyboard picture for correct fingering. Type each line 3 times, saying each letter before typing it.

G   asdfgf fgf gfgf fig gas guess gig give gave

        gale sage fog log lag wag gag pig goal gold

T   asdfgtg gtg tgtg ftf tftf told tattle time tire

        tissue meet seat site cattle kettle jilt soft

B   asdfgbfg fbfbf bfbf biff fiber bug fob but fgbgtf

        gtgbg fibbed bored fable bomb bud bulb big bifocal

H   ;lkjhj jhj hjhj hale has his huff laugh the

     had have ham wham who whose hap halter halve half

Y   ;lkjhyhj jhyhj jyj yjyj yes yale yard happy

     yet year silly very city boy merry jolly

N   ;lkjhnh jhyhnhj jnj njnj nanny jangle sun funny

     fine winning swinging and suction action lane

REVIEW: abcde fghij klmno pqrst uvwxy z;,./

You now know all the letters of the alphabet.

Shift Key

To type a capital letter, you hold down the shift key while striking the letter key. Follow this sequence for a capital A:

1. Hold down the shift key on the *right-hand* side of the typewriter with your right little finger.

2. Strike the A with your little finger on the left hand.

3. Release the shift key.

Remember you need *two* hands for a capital. You use the shift key on the opposite side of the keyboard from the letter key. You always use your little finger to hold the shift down.

Now type the following lines once:

     Fay. Jerry. Kevin. Dick. Sally.

     Edward. Carl. Victor. Harry.

     Gloria. Izzie. Betty. Leo. Mary.

     Ned. Ann. Orson. Peter. Richie.

     Ted. Zed. William.

     ;?; ?;? Who is it? Is it Leo?

     Is it Ted? It is I. What is your name?

     My name is ....

Look at your watch or a clock and note the time. Then type this paragraph 3 times. Say each letter aloud before typing it.

She fed him a pair of red jell peppers; he moved quickly and seized the big jar. The full fugue uses an extra dull tune. What is it like?

Circle your errors. If you have at least 15 words correct in any one paragraph, go on to Step 5. Otherwise, take a break and try typing the paragraph again. If you typed the paragraph in 7 minutes, you were typing at the rate of 4 words a minute. If you needed 5 minutes, you typed 6 words a minute.

Step 5

Objective: To build your typing speed.

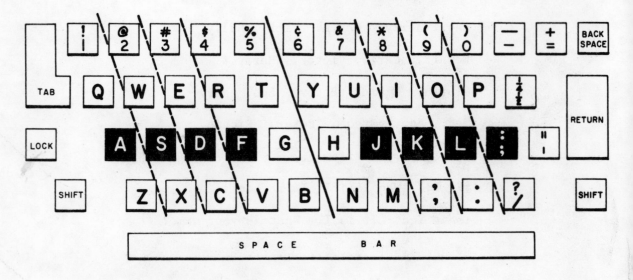

Type each line 3 times as quickly as you can:

The owl and the dog go down the bicycle paths together.

The chaps with their torn socks roam the city and town.

Sue and Bob got an authentic antique bus for the visit.

Pamela signs her name with a pencil; I sign with a pen.

She laughed when he said he wished she had a busy job.

Read the following paragraphs first and then type them as quickly as possible. Remember to hit the space bar *2 times* between sentences. Say every letter aloud before typing it.

Learning good technique in typing requires immediate emphasis on speed. It is a motor skill which needs to be developed, not intellectualized. Your fingers are not familiar with the actions necessary for typing, so you must train them to strike the keys with a fast motion like a bullet. This can be harder to do than just learning the keyboard.

After your fingers become faster, you will be able to direct them more accurately. Remember when you first learned to dance and your feet did not go quite where you wanted them? Learning to type is the same: speed and rhythm first and then you will refine your stroking for accuracy. First push for speed until you have made substantial gains. The next day slow down for accuracy.

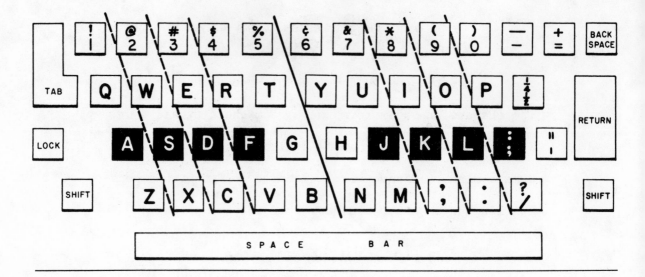

Try to force your speed by typing faster than is

comfortable. Do not even look at errors at this time

as no one can concentrate on speed and accuracy at the

same time. You can work on your accuracy later. In

fact, unless you make errors during speed practice, you

are not typing fast enough to benefit from the practice.

Before you finish this book, you will work on accuracy. Now concentrate on speed.

Take a 5-minute break to stretch before continuing with this lesson.

Here's more copy to type to strengthen your fingers. Type it as fast as you can. Say every letter aloud before typing it so you control your fingers and keep your mind on what you are typing.

How to Time Your Typing

You will probably want to know how fast you are typing.

To find out, have someone time you with a watch or clock

with a sweep second hand on the special copy you

will find in the next lesson.

You can also make your own timer by using any tape recorder. First, put a one minute timing on tape by saying, For one minute, start typing. Then, after one minute has elapsed according to your clock, say, One minute, stop typing. Make three one minute timings on the tape, one right after the other.

Then, make three five minute timings on the tape in the same way. Say, For five minutes, start typing. At each minute mark, announce the minutes, such as One minute, Two minutes, Three minutes, Four minutes, Five minutes, stop typing.

Did you type this lesson in one hour or less?
If so, you are typing very fast for a beginner.

Step 6

Objectives: To time your typing.
To set a goal of speed or accuracy.

You'll take your first timing in this lesson. Make a timing tape as outlined in Step 5 or use a clock with a sweep second hand. The tape is easier to use because you can hear it rather than having to keep looking up at the clock.

After you get setup with your timer, set narrow margins (1 inch) so you will have a 65 space line for typing. Then type the 5 sentences given at the beginning of Step 5 as quickly as you can for 10 minutes. This is used as a warm up for your fingers.

POSITION CHECK: Feet flat on floor, typewriter squarely in front of you.

Keep your eyes on your copy and avoid looking at the keyboard if possible after your fingers are anchored on the home row.

Say every letter aloud before typing it.

Speed is important.

When you have typed for 10 to 15 minutes, you're ready to take a few timings of 1-minute each. Take three 1-minute timings, one right after the other with no time in between. Start each timing with a new line of the copy below. Type for speed.

A sunny day in spring is a glorious, glorious time of year.

People bring out their bicycles to ride and bask in the sun.

Girls and boys go running down the street after runaway dogs.

Men and women gather on the sunny side to enjoy the warm sun.

The yellow and red tulips and pink azaleas are in full bloom.

The sky is very blue and there is no wind to blow the clouds.

How many words did you type per minute? Count the words in each timing. There are approximately 12 words on each of the above lines. Keep a record of your speed so you can watch your improvement with each day's timing.

Speed or Accuracy?

If you typed for 1 minute with 4 or fewer incorrect words, your goal should be speed.

If you had 5 or more words mistyped, your goal is accuracy. Slow down and be sure to say each letter aloud before you type it. If you really feel insecure with the keyboard, review Step 4.

How to Figure Speed

You will notice that we counted only 1 error per word. Also, when figuring typing speeds, every 5 strokes and spaces are counted as 1 word. On unmarked copy, you can count the number of strokes and spaces and divide by 5 to get the total number of words. Then to figure the words per minute, divide the number of words by the number of minutes you typed.

Keep a separate count of your words per minute and your errors. This way you can tell whether your goal for that lesson is speed or accuracy. You will find, however, when you apply for a job that many times the employer testing you will subtract your total errors from your words per minute to get a net speed. Also, 5-minute timings are generally used for employment tests. You'll have a chance to test your typing on longer timings later on in the book.

Typing Progress Chart

DATE	GOAL IS		WORDS A MINUTE	ERRORS	LENGTH OF TIMING
	SPEED	ACCURACY			

If your goal is *speed,* type each of the following lines 3 times. If your goal is *accuracy,* type the following paragraphs 3 times.

The best acre was saved for Caesar. Eve saw Rex; and Rex saw Eve.

Are cars ready for Eva and Ted? Do you care if we have eggs?

Save the best date after the seventh of September for Caesar.

It was an extra great farce with dazed deers and daffy zebras.

The rage for the dwarf cedar trees grew. Does Wes care for beer?

We were eating a feast of bread and water in the cafe terrace.

If your goal is speed or accuracy, strive
for that in typing this material:

Library of Information and Research: Your Files.

Files are just a logical, consistent way of keeping material

so you can always find it quickly and easily. There are

several ways of filing things depending upon the needs of your

particular office. Generally, incoming correspondence is

filed under the last name of the persons writing the letter

or the name of their companies. Outgoing correspondence

would be filed under the name of the person to whom the

letter is addressed or the company name. In the file

folder, you will have all correspondence to or from this

company or person in chronological order with the most

recent letter on top. Staples or large clips are usually

used to keep it all together.

Other ways to file information would be by subject or

account number. You can look through your files and

discover very easily which system you should use.

Some people like to keep what is called a reading file in addition to the other files. This consists of carbons of letters sent out in chronological order, the most recent on top. Many times this is kept in just a three ringed binder.

A tickler file to tickle your memory is helpful. Have a manila folder for each day of the month and put notes for follow up under the appropriate date. Maybe you will want to remind your boss two days before an important meeting to get specific information ready for it. Or perhaps you are collecting material for a special meeting to be held at the end of the month. You could keep this in one of these folders, or you could jot a note on your calendar. Make it work for you.

An address and telephone file is vital for you and, of course, your boss. You may want to have a company card with all your contacts in that one company in it and then also have the persons listed under their individual names. Remember to keep this up to date as you go along.

From all your research and work in libraries, you are familiar with the way things are alphabetized. One rule you might want to remember is that nothing goes before something: Woods, Robert, goes before Woods, Robert M.

Step 7

Objectives: To increase your speed.
To learn how to center titles and names.

Warm up on the following drills for the
left and right hands for 15 minutes. Say
every letter before you type it.

Few red cars are seen by zebras.   The cars are in garages.

The cat ate the leaves of grass.   The red setter was full.

An average secretary types fifty words a minute accurately.

In my opinion bright and sunny Honolulu is a great place.

Millions of people like nylon pompoms.   Do you like them?

Jimmy jumps high with joy when Polly jumps upon the moon.

1-Minute Timings

for Speed

Now you are ready to try three 1-minute
timings. Start each timing with the new
sentence. Say every letter before you type
it and go as fast as you can.

Learning to type takes lots of concentration and hard work.

Every five strokes count as one word in figuring your speed.

You have a sense of freedom when you can type your own papers.

If you can type well, you can get a job anywhere in the world.

When you type, you can put all information into the computers.

A beautifully typed page, well placed on the paper, is an art.

Each of the lines above is counted as 12
words. Compute your speed for each 1-
minute timing. Did you go faster than in
Step 6? Enter your speed on your progress
chart.

Speed Copy

Type the following copy for speed. Say
each letter a little faster than your fingers
can type comfortably.

Travel Arrangements. Before your bosses leave on a trip, be
sure they have all the papers and information they will need
for their meetings and enough money for expenses. They may
need a travel advance. You will want to type up appointment
schedules for them and itineraries showing airlines, flight
numbers, departure and arrival times, and the airports involved.
If they are planning to leave cars at the airport make sure
that they return to the same airport. Pogostick is the hard
way to get across town. You will want to keep copies of
these itineraries. You may need still other copies for
people in the office.

Most offices have a copy of the Official Airline Guide which
lists schedules for all airlines. The quick reference edition
lists schedules for the airlines in an easy to read format.

Large companies have a travel department to make reservations
and do the ticketing. In smaller offices, you will be asked
to make the reservations and pick up the tickets yourself.
Your boss may have an air travel card which you can use to
charge the tickets. Other offices may make all their travel
arrangements through a travel agency. Here, your ability to
communicate and to get along well with others will help
you get the flights and the service that your boss wants.

How to Center

First, determine the center of your paper by folding it in half (right edge to left edge) and crease it lightly at the top.

Then put the paper in your machine so that the center of your paper is at the center mark on your typewriter scale. This is usually marked with a line or an arrow. Once you get your paper in the typewriter, set your paper guide (the sliding piece of metal on the left-hand side of the roller) to be sure the next sheet of paper is at the same spot.

To center your name, just follow these steps:

1. Go to the center of your paper.

2. Backspace once for every two letters and spaces in your name. If there is an odd letter left over, don't count it.

3. Now type your name.

Is your name in the center of the page? If not, try again, following the directions exactly.

For practice, type the following title page, centering each line on the page. Also, try to center the titles up and down on the page so that there are just a few more lines at the bottom of the menu than at the top. (There are a total of 66 lines on a page 8½″ × 11″ on both pica and elite typewriters.)

Does your page look like the reduced version at right? If not, try again following the directions for centering step by step.

ROMEO AND JULIET

by

William Shakespeare

Directed by

Gregory G. Gauntlett

Produced by

Nancy C. Kirkpatrick

Costumes by

Martin Misterivitch

ROMEO AND JULIET

by

William Shakespeare

Directed by

Gregory G. Gauntlett

Produced by

Nancy C. Kirkpatrick

Costumes by

Martin Misterivitch

Step 8

Objectives: To learn number keys.
To learn punctuations and mark symbol keys.
To learn use of tab key.

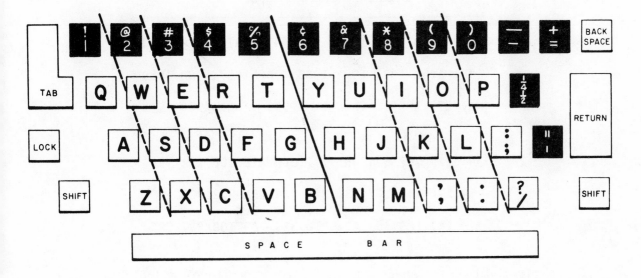

Numbers

Learn what fingers to use on the number keys and learn to type them without looking. This way you will always be able to gain speed when typing many numbers.

Place your hands in home-row position. Now move both hands up to the number row on a diagonal slightly to the left. Your little fingers are anchored on 0 on the right and I on the left.

Note: Some manual typewriters use a small I for the number 1 and a capital O for zero. In these cases your index fingers are on the same keys as on electric typewriters – 4 and 7.

Refer to keyboard diagram for confirmation of your fingering.

Type each line 2 times. Say each letter and number aloud.

444 333 222 111 666 555 777 888 999 000

898 789 909 707 808 767 676 868 969

1234567890 1234567890 1234567890 1234567890

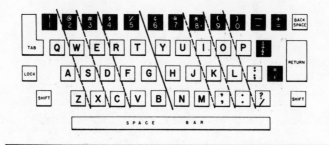

```
1972 1973 1974 1975 1976 1977 1978 1979 1980

1981 1982 1983 1984 1985 1986 1987 1988 1989

May 27, 1987.  This is 1999.  June 1900.


384 279 482 394 687 777 010 111 000 222 999

759 274 249 147 981 721 964 161 802 300 400

710 147 183 502 472 710 329 789 100 297 395


fr4r fgt5tg ju7uj hy6yh de3ed ki8ik sw2ws lo9ol aqlqa ;p0p;
```

Punctuation Marks and Symbols

You should learn to use punctuation marks easily and quickly, since they will occur very frequently in your typing. You should also learn where the symbols are, but it is not necessary to gain as much speed typing them unless they appear often in the material you are typing.

Refer to the keyboard diagram for the correct fingering for your typewriter.

Repeat each of the exercises for the punctuation marks and symbols until you can type each line without looking and with only one or two errors. Say each letter, mark, or symbol aloud to force concentration and to develop a smooth, even rhythm.

APOSTROPHE ('): On an electric typewriter, the apostrophe is on the right side next to ;. Use your right little finger. Remember to move the little finger only. Leave the other fingers on home-row position.

On a manual typewriter, the apostrophe is over the 8 key. Use right hand, second finger (k-finger). Shift with left hand, little finger.

```
a;lki8 li'k k'k a;'; ;'; ''' s's es' let's George's
```

You can put in as many different tab stops as you want, at any place, and you can take them out as often as you like.

If your carriage did not go directly to the center, there are probably tab stops already in your typewriter. Let's take them out. Here's how:

1. Return carriage to left margin.

2. Push TAB key.

3. When carriage stops, push key marked "CLEAR."

4. Repeat this procedure until the entire line is clear. Now you can put in the tabs where you want them.

Notice that "tabs" are stops between the left and right margins. You can set as many tabs as there are spaces. To set your left and right margins follow the directions for specific typewriters.

HOW TO INDENT AND INDICATE PARAGRAPHS

To indent for paragraphs, you will use the tab key. You will usually indent five spaces from the left margin. Return your carriage to the left margin. Tap the space bar five times and push SET key.

Now each time you want to indent from the left margin, push TAB key once. This is faster than striking the space bar five times.

When paragraphs are single spaced, they may be started at the margin or may be indented five spaces. You will always use a double space between each paragraph.

When paragraphs are double spaced, you can double or triple space between paragraphs. When you double space between paragraphs, you will always indent the first line. When you triple space between paragraphs, you may start at the margin or you may indent five spaces.

Instructions for typing the material you have just read:

1. Center the heading "TABS."

2. Clear all the tabs in your machine now.

3. Take carriage to 5 spaces in from left margin and set a tab.

4. Move carriage another 5 spaces and set another tab.

5. Set line space indicator on single space.

6. Single space the material with double spaces between paragraphs.

7. Type the sections "TABS" and "HOW TO INDENT AND INDICATE PARA-GRAPHS."

Step 9

for speed

Objectives: To improve your typing accuracy.
To take a 5-minute timing.
To learn how to type manuscripts.

Accuracy

Accuracy is your goal today. Slow down your typing speed a little and try to be as accurate as possible. Say every letter aloud before typing it. *Concentrate* on each let-ter. Type the following copy for accuracy.

Do not time yourself. Do not type the aster-isks or the numbers at the end of the lines.

Reports, articles, term papers, stories are usually* typed in   (10)

manuscript form. The manuscript should* be easy to read and   (20)

accurate. If the typing is well* placed on the page, you will   (30)

be inviting the* reader to concentrate on your subject matter.   (40)

Manuscripts* are usually double spaced in the body. The*   (50/60)

footnotes and quotations are single spaced. Paragraphs* are   (70)

indented five spaces. The pages are* numbered one inch from   (80)

the bottom of the page in the* center. The page number is pre-   (90)

ceded and followed* by a hyphen. Your manuscript can be stapled   (100)

at* the top or side or it can be bound in an attractive* cover   (110/120)

which usually clips on the left side.*   (130)

Your margins should be wide. A one and a half inch* margin is a   (140)

good width. However, if you are binding* your report on the left   (150)

side, you will want to make* it wider, such as two inches. A   (160)

trick to be* sure that your typing is centered as you want it is*   (170/180)

to use a backing sheet immediately behind the paper* you are typing   (190)

on. On the backing sheet outline* in heavy black ink your margins.   (200)

This way you* will know where to start and stop typing.   (210)

If you* have one and a half inch margins, you will have 24* lines   (220/230)

of copy on your page. You begin typing on* line 10 and stop typ-   (240)

ing on line 58. Your page number* goes on line 63 which is half   (250)

an inch from the* bottom of the page. There are a total of 66 lines*(260/270)

on a sheet of paper 11 inches long.*   (277)

After you have typed the above copy, circle each word with a mistake. Then write the incorrect letters in the right margin and the letter which should have been typed next to it. Have you made the same mistake several times or just made random errors?

On the blank keyboard picture, write in the letters you had trouble typing correctly. Then select the drills for those letters from the letter substitution drills on the following pages. Type each line 3 times and say each letter aloud before typing it.

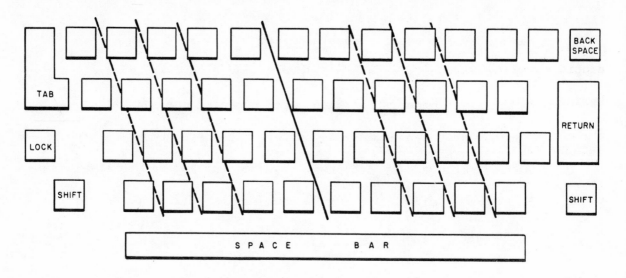

Letter Substitution Drills

A–E:
great active escape break erratic scenario racer potential

manageable malfeasance

A–S:
asks mayonnaise manuscripts sandblasts scandals scalawags

saxophones
A–Z:
zebra zealous zigzagged glamorized realize actualize

B–G:
big bag gabby boggle grabbed gable gamble boondoggle

B–N:
bin been beneath noble notable nimble hobnail bean

B—V:
believe volleyball overboard vagabond bonvivant bivalve vocabulary

38

C–D:
cedar cried reached dog catcher docile discern discover discotheque

C–S:
such search cheese sick chases chooses choices cherish decisive

sandwiches classical social scenic sarcastic stick plastic

C–V:
vice curve victory cursive culvert viscous vocal volcanic

C–X:
exotic extras excel exact excite except exclaim executive

Mexican xenophobic xebec excellence

D–E:
details determine dewdrop educated devastated edited editor edelweiss

D–F:
daffy definite differ find fuddy duddy fad fiddle faddle fat feed feet

D–K:
dark duck dock kidding kind kindred liked licked kindling kingdom

D–S:
scandalous swindled sandwich scheduled leads dreams dizziness

E–I:
receive believe variety material kaiser conceive time heir their friend

E–O:
woe theory thereof thereupon foreign opulence orientation outrageous

E–R:
rejoice reinforce correspondence correlate corporate relegate scenery

E–S:
easy easier easiest finest disburse increase persist persons

E–T:
bet get better letter the entertainer there their ten stretch

E–W:
we were wed Wednesday when we were weary but wealthy and wise.

F–G:
forgive forgot forget grateful fugitive fugue glassful goffer

F–R:
ruff free further frankfurter flower refer reflex proffering refresh

G–H:
though thought taught right high hag haggle hedge hog hoggish hug

H–J:
heebie-jeebies hung jury Jehovah jack-hammer John

I–K:
ilk kickoff khaki kilometer kaleidoscope katydid kindness kinetic

I–O:
social spoil void interior mastoid ionize violate kilocycle

I–U:
unit unique infuse inaugurate inauspicious habitual gullible
nautical uniform

K–L:
luck lake like lark knowledge kilowatt kilometer kindliness milk

L–O:
low lovable mobile gallon saloon salon oil original

M–N:
man mundane municipal pamper painter monkey name mission numerous

O–P:
open piccolo pigeon opium flop blow-pipe purpose proud

O–U:
ouch utopia journal juror goulash gouache vaporous upshot

P–Q:
quip quipped equip piquant perquisite quadruple quintuplet

R–T:
tree treat trivet tract there their roster retrieve rest

R–U:
runner rural route particular parquet mural murmurous

S–W:
sweet saw waist swoop straw weeks worship twists west swear

T–Y:
yet type typify yeast activity hasty festivity neutrally yogurt

U–Y:
nutty buddy nursery gratuity gratuitous usually tutelary turkey

. – , :
red, yellow...orange, pink...green, blue...purple, black...

Type these drills whenever you find yourself substituting one letter for another.

Go back to the copy at the beginning of Step 9 which you typed for accuracy. You will now type it again to see how few errors you make in 5 minutes. Set your tape or timer for 5 minutes. Do not type the asterisks or numbers at the end of the lines.

HOW TO FIGURE YOUR ACCURACY:

Circle each word with an error. Only one error per word is counted. Enter the total errors on your chart. At this stage, if you have only 7 or 8 errors on a 5-minute timing, you are doing very well. Eventually, you will want to reduce your errors on a timing to 1 or less per minute.

HOW TO FIGURE TYPING SPEED:

On each timing, count the number of letters and spaces you typed beyond the last asterisk. Divide this number by 5 to get your additional words. (Remember, 5 letters and spaces count as 1 word.) Add these words to the word count at the last asterisk for your total word count.

On the 5-minute timings, divide by 5 (minutes) to get your speed per minute. Enter your speeds on your timing chart.

For example, if you typed through "Your margins should be wide." on a 5-minute timing, figure your typing speed as follows:

Additional letters and spaces	28
Divide by 5	5 ⌐28
Additional words	6
Add word count at last asterisk	130
Total words typed	136
Divide by 5 minutes	5 ⌐136
Words per minute	27

How to Type Manuscripts

The material which you have just typed on your 5-minute timing gives you a general idea about manuscript typing. (Read it over again if you don't remember what it said.) Make a backing sheet as described in it.

In the following report, which you will type, note that the title on the first page begins on line 10. Leave 4 lines between the second line of the title and the text. On the second and succeeding pages, start on the text on line 10. Triple space between paragraphs.

The first page of the report is typed exactly as you should type it if you are using the same size type. The other pages are marked with corrections which you should make as you type them. The standard proofreader's marks are shown below:

C̲	Capitalize	Let it stand	STAND STET
⁄	Lower case (small letter)	Transpose	hte
		Space	#
⊏	Move left	Close up	⊃
⊐	Move right	Paragraph	¶
⊓	Move up	No new	
⊔	Move down	paragraph	No new ¶
∧	Insert	Delete, take out	ℓ
__	Underscore or italicize	Spell out	sp or (20th)

THROUGH RAIN AND SNOW, SUN AND RAIN:

THE U.S. MAIL

Incoming Mail

Nine o'clock, and the mail is waiting for you. Opening
the mail is important to do as soon as you get to the office.
As you open each envelope, be sure that you take out everything and that there is a return address on the letter. Some
organizations like to have the letters stamped with the date
you receive them. Put the most important first class mail
on top; then, the interoffice memos, then ads, magazines and
newspapers.

Read all the mail over, so you'll know what's happening.
If any of the letters or memos refer to previous correspondence,
pull the old correspondence from the file and attach it to the
letter so your bosses will have all the information they need
at their fingertips. You'll probably enjoy reading over the
newspapers and magazines and marking any special articles for
your bosses's attention. You can be a real assistant in this
way.

Put all the incoming mail in manila folders. Mark
them "Incoming Mail" on the front of the folder, and put them
on your bosses's desks so it will be there when they get in.

42

The folders keep the mail all in a neat pile and also keeps it away from curious eyes.

Special Note: Sometimes your bosses will get mail marked "personal and confidential" or will get mail that obviously looks personal. Unless they tell you otherwise, leave these unopened.

Triple Space

Outgoing Mail

Triple Space

The proof of your skill at the typewriter is a beautiful letter ready for signature. As you finish each letter, put the letter to be signed with its envelope together with the carbon copy and the letter being answered, all clipped together in a manila folder marked, "For Your Signature." Don't forget to mark the envelopes with any special instructions such as "Air Mail" or "personal and Confidential." As memos are used exclusively for correspondence within an office, use interoffice envelopes for these.

Packages or large reports or really anything that would go in a 9 x 12 envelope will need an address label. Most companies will have printed address lables for you to type.

Usually company mailrooms wrap packages, stamp envelopes on a postage meter, and even seal the envelopes. You'll have an "out" basket on your desk where you will put all material for the mailroom and it will be picked up seyral times dring

the day. Occasionaly, you might need to send out a letter or

a package after the mailrom has closed at nigt. In such

emeriencies, there are usually stamps at the reception desk

or some other convenient location. If not, you maywant to

keep some on hand for just such an emergency.

    Zip codes really do speed the mail on its way. Put

the Zip code just one space after the state using no perod

or comma.[1]

---

[1]Use the official U. S. Post Office abbreviations for the
states.

44

Step 10

Objective: To learn to type letters.

You'll notice that at the beginning of each step you've typed some material to warm up, to get fingers moving the way you want, whether for speed or accuracy. In this step, you will learn about typing letters, which, of course, should be accurate.

Therefore, type the following material for accuracy. Say each letter aloud before typing it so you can control your fingers. Try to type it with less than 5 errors. Retype the material if necessary. A score of 3 (or less) errors is excellent.

Why should I learn to type? I am looking for a job and I want the

best one I can get with more pay and better opportunities. I

want a job using brains and education. And, while I am in school,

I want to be able to type my papers, my thesis and to get a part-

time job. Also, neater homework papers should help me get better

marks. I am a homemaker and I want to improve my typing before re-

turning to the business world. Maybe I will even get a part-time

job when Sally starts school next fall. I have a job now, but I

would like a better one, one with a higher salary and that requires

faster typing. I want to type because I am a reporter and I

must be able to get out stories quickly and have them readable.

It is a real accomplishment to learn to type and I am doing it.

How to Type Letters

The main purpose of a letter is to communicate with someone else, to tell them something, to ask them to do something. Because you want the person receiving the letter to be open to what you are saying and to consider your suggestions and ideas, you want the other person to read it. Do all you can to make your typing readable.

A short line of text is usually easier to read. A newspaper column, for example, is much faster to read than a magazine article that goes across a full page. The same with the letter. You'll want the margins on each side of the letter to balance, in other words, to be equal (just as the margins at the top and the bottom should be equal).

Assume the letterhead you use is 8½″ × 11″.

1. The margins on both sides should be 1½″ to 2″.

   • *For pica type* (the larger type with 10 characters to the inch):

   a. If the edge of your paper starts at 0, you would set your left margin at 15 for a 1½″ margin (10 × 1½ = 15) or at 20 for a 2″ margin (10 × 2 = 20).

   b. If the center of your typewriter is 0, be sure the center of your paper is at 0. This puts the left and right edges of your paper at 42. In this case, a 1½″ margin would be at 27 (42 − 15 as in *a* above). A 2″ margin would be at 22 (42 − 20 as in *a* above).

   c. Your right margin would be set an equal number of spaces from the right edge of your paper. If the right edge of your paper is at 85, a 1½″ margin should be set at 70, a 2″ margin at 65.

   • *For elite type* (smaller type with 12 characters to the inch):

   a. If the edge of your paper starts at 0, set your left margin at 18 for a 1½″ margin (12 × 1¼ = 18) or at 24 for a 2″ margin (12 × 2 = 24).

   b. If the center of your typewriter is 0, be sure the center of your paper is at 0. This puts the eges of your paper at 51. In this case, a 1½″ margin would be at 33 (51 − 18 as *a* above), a 2″ margin at 27.

   c. Your right margin would be set an equal number of spaces from the right edge of your paper. If the right edge of your paper is at 102, a 1½″ margin should be set at 84, a 2″ margin at 78.

You may find that you want to set your right margin 3 to 5 spaces closer to the edge. The warning bell on the right side of your typewriter is often set so early that you leave the line too short and your margins will not balance.

2. The average place to start your dateline is 15 lines down from the top edge of the paper. If the letter is very long, start the date higher. If it is very short, start the date lower.

3. Start the date at the center of your page. Keep a tab set at the center.

4. Come down 5 or 6 lines from the date to start the inside address. This number of lines can vary depending on the length of the letter.

5. Type the inside name and address at the left margin. This should be single spaced. Always be sure to use a title with a name: Mr., Mrs., Miss, Ms., Dr., etc.

6. Spell out street, avenue, etc. The state may be abbreviated, using the latest U.S. Post Office-approved abbreviations (such as NY for New York, CT for Connecticut). Use capitals and no period. The state is followed by a space, and then the zip code is typed.

7. Allow one blank line between the inside name and address and the salutation (Dear Mr. Jones). This is called double spacing. There is always only a double space in this spot. This spacing does not vary.

8. The salutation in a business letter is followed by a colon.

9. Double space between the salutation and the body of the letter. This spacing does not vary.

10. The block form is generally used for a business letter. This means no indentations for paragraphs, single spacing the text, and double spacing between each paragraph. This spacing does not vary.

11. Between the last line of the text and the complimentary close, double space. This spacing does not vary.

12. The complimentary close (Sincerely, Very truly yours) is started at the center mark of your paper. Use a tab for this.

13. The number of lines you leave for the signature will depend on the writer's handwriting. The standard number is 4 or 6.

14. Start typing the name of the person signing the letter at the center, as you did the closing.

15. If you are using a title, type this directly under the name.

16. The initials of the writer of the letter are typed in capital letters at the margin, one or more lines below the name. This is followed by a colon and the typist's initials in small letters. No periods are used and there is no space between the letters.

17. An enclosure in a letter is shown immediately below the reference initials:

    BO: es
    Enc.   (3)

    This indicates three enclosures.

18. The names of the persons getting carbon copies are given below the enclosure notation. Do not indicate file copies, since keeping them is standard procedure.

19. Occasionally you will want to send a carbon of a letter to someone but will not want that information to show on the original. These are called *blind carbons.* In this case, take the original letter out of the typewriter and type the notation on the carbons only:

    bc: Joseph Boganovitch

20. A postscript is a note at the end of a letter. It is typed block-style under the last notation:

    BO: es
    Enc.   (3)
    cc: Dan Strong
    bc: Joseph Boganovitch
    P.S. A postscript can be used to emphasize a very important idea in the letter.

21. *Proofread* and make any necessary corrections *before* you take the letter out of the typewriter.

First type the sample letter shown on page 48. Then type the following letters in standard block form. Be sure to correct spelling and punctuation. Use your dictionary!

Aim for mailable letters—ones which you would be happy to sign. Any correction should be almost invisible.

Proofread before taking your letter out of the typewriter.

After typing each letter, check it with the correctly typed letter shown in miniature after the text of the four letters.

BETTY OWEN

SECRETARIAL SYSTEMS, INC.

630 THIRD AVENUE AT 41st STREET
NEW YORK, NEW YORK 10017
212/867-7667

October 23, 19--

Miss Jane McCormick
310 East 55th Street
New York, NY 10022

Dear Miss McCormick:

You will be considered a skilled typist if you can set up
and type a "good looking" letter. No matter how long it
takes you, the final result is what counts.

Think of a letter as a picture. You want to frame it and
make it easy to read. For this reason, you will want wide
margins to leave plenty of white space. This gives
importance to the letter.

The margins and spacing are indicated for this letter.
For longer or shorter ones, raise or lower them on the page.
Unless the letter is unusually short or long, the margins
stay the same.

Be an artist and have fun typing your "picture."

                    Sincerely,

                    Betty Owen

BO:urs
cc: Mr. Smith

Notice the punctuation is *inside* the quotation marks.

Remember: *Proofread* before taking the letter out of the typewriter.

Date, Mrs. Benjamin Robinson, Jojo Paperbacks Inc., 3333333345 Madison Avenue, New York, NY 10022 Dear Mrs. Robinson: Congratulations! The city couldn't have elected a more deserving "MOTHER OF THE YEAR!" I know that you have and will continue to amply fulfill this most distinguished title.

The best of luck to you in this new and important assignment. Sincerely, Amantha Wailing Wall. AWW:urs

Date, Mr. Orville Wright, Lenox Hill Hospital, Park Avenue and 77th Street, New York, NY 10021 Dear Orville: Congratulations! They told us that it would never fly, but you, my dear friend, have done it! I have every confidence that the fuselage can be adequately reinforced with coat hangers.

We must get together once you have recovered from the unfortunate accident. Sincerely, Wilbur Wright. WW:urs

Date, Miss Laura Prentiss, 42 Avon Place, Mamaroneck, NY

10543 Dear Miss Prentiss: When you were in to see me on

your spring vacation, I had nothing open in the way of an

editorial position here, and I was sorry I could not be

encouraging.

The personnel scene is always changing, however, and a

great job for someone with your college background has come

up. If you had not passed the typing test, I would not be

able to offer it to you, but I think you would enjoy the job.

And certainly we would like to have you here.

It is in the Special Books Division, working with Mr.

Taylor, formerly with Time Magazine, Inc. Could you possibly

come in tomorrow or the next day to meet and talk with him?

Sincerely, Richard S. Benson, Personnel Director. RSB:urs

Date, Mr. Elijah Elephant, Cage 12, Block A, The Mellifluous

Zoo, Philibuster, Cantankerous Dear Mr. Elephant: The other

day I met a very close friend of yours: Mr. Fenimore Foxe.

He informed me of your present difficulties with your keeper.

I understand that the keeper's son is passionately fond of

peanuts, and so what little supply you have is constantly

diminishing.

The only solution seems to be replacement of either the son

or the keeper. Since the former is presently inconvenient,

I'm afraid it will have to be the latter. Please inform me
if this will be satisfactory. As you know, we try to take
every precaution to ensure our guests a pleasant time.
Sincerely, Trimble Titmouse, Director of Zoo Residence.
TT:urs

June 19, 19--

June 15, 19--

Mrs. Benjamin Robinson
Jojo Paperbacks Inc.
3333333345 Madison Avenue
New York, NY 10022

Dear Mrs. Robinson:

Congratulations! The city couldn't have elected a
more deserving "MOTHER OF THE YEAR!" I know
that you have and will continue to amply fulfill this
most distinguished title.

The best of luck to you in this new and important
assignment.

Sincerely,

Amantha Wailing Wall

AWW:urs

Mr. Orville Wright
Lenox Hill Hospital
Park Avenue and 77th Street
New York, NY 10021

Dear Orville:

Congratulations! They told us that it would never
fly, but you, my dear friend, have done it! I have
every confidence that the fuselage can be adequately
reinforced with coat hangers.

We must get together once you have recovered from
the unfortunate accident.

Sincerely,

Wilbur Wright

WW:urs

June 15, 19--

June 15, 19--

Miss Laura Prentiss
42 Avon Place
Mamaroneck, NY 10543

Dear Miss Prentiss:

When you were in to see me on your spring
vacation, I had nothing open in the way of
an editorial position here, and I was sorry
I could not be encouraging.

The personnel scene is always changing,
however, and a great job for someone with
your college background has come up. If you
had not passed the typing test, I would not be
able to offer it to you, but I think you would
enjoy the job. And certainly we would like
to have you here.

It is in the Special Books Division, working
with Mr. Taylor, formerly with Time Magazine,
Inc. Could you possibly come in tomorrow or
the next day to meet and talk with him?

Sincerely,

Richard S. Benson
Personnel Director

RSB:urs

Mr. Elijah Elephant
Cage 12, Block A
The Mellifluous Zoo
Philibuster, Cantankerous

Dear Mr. Elephant:

The other day I met a very close friend
of yours: Mr. Fenimore Foxe. He informed
me of your present difficulties with your
keeper. I understand that the keeper's
son is passionately fond of peanuts, and
so what little supply you have is constantly
diminishing.

The only solution seems to be replacement of
either the son or the keeper. Since the
former is presently inconvenient, I'm afraid
it will have to be the latter. Please inform
me if this will be satisfactory. As you
know, we try to take every precaution to
ensure our guests a pleasant time.

Sincerely,

Trimble Titmouse
Director of Zoo Residence

TT:urs

Type the following copy to learn how envelopes are addressed. Your goal is accuracy.

The standard business envelope is usually a No. 9 or a

No. 10. The standard letterhead is 8-1/2 inches by 11 inches

and is folded in thirds to go in the envelope.

TO FOLD A LETTER 8½"x11" FOR
AN ENVELOPE NO.9 OR NO.10

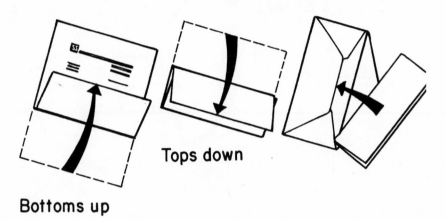

Tops down

Bottoms up

When addressing the envelope, use block style. For a

three-line address, double space. For a four-line address,

single space. Always type the city, state, and zip code on one

line.

For a No. 10 envelope, start the address on line 14,

about 4 inches from the left edge. Or, if you keep a

center tab stop in your typewriter, use that as a margin for

envelopes.

Special mailing instructions such as registered or air mail should be typed in all capital letters below the stamp area.

Notations such as "PERSONAL AND CONFIDENTIAL" and "Attention: Mr. Sam Smith" are typed to the left side of the envelope, below the address.

GROSSET & DUNLAP, INC.
PUBLISHERS

51 MADISON AVENUE, NEW YORK, NEW YORK 10010

REGISTERED

Mrs. Mary Mansfield
Center for Urban Education
300 Madison Avenue
New York, NY 10017

PERSONAL AND CONFIDENTIAL

other things you should know

You will probably want to continue to improve your typing. You can do this by following the directions given in this section. Read the material for information and then type it for practice.

The numbers at the end of the lines show the total words in that selection to the asterisk(s) on that line. Do not type the asterisks or the timing figures. Refer to Step 6 for figuring your speed.

HOW TO INCREASE YOUR SPEED FROM HERE

Practice and more practice. Each time you type,* be sure   (10)

you have a goal in mind. Today, is it* to be speed or accuracy?   (20)

Remember, research has* shown that you cannot concentrate on*   (30/40) both at the same time. Select one or the other for* each   (50)

session of typing.

Typing is a skill which* must be exercised. Self-discipline   (60)

will be needed* to increase your speed and improve your accuracy.*   (70/80)

Type following these suggestions:

1. Set a* definite time each day to practice.   (90)

2. Set a goal* of speed or accuracy each day.   (100)

3. Say every* letter aloud before typing it so that you   (110)

    control* your fingers.   (120)

4. When working on speed, really* push yourself.   (130)

5. For copy, use material in this* book over again or any   (140)

    other material which is* easy to read.   (150)

6. Keep a record of your progress,* showing the dates,   (160)

    speed, and number of errors.* You'll have good days and   (170)

    off days, but the* overall movement will be good.   (180)

7. Persevere.* Learning to type can be fun, frustrating,   (190)

    difficult,* and rewarding. However, you must keep doing   (200)

    it--it* just takes time to reach your goals. But you   (210)

    can* do it!   (220)

Good luck!

HOW TO TAKE TESTS

Relax. That's the secret to* any test-taking, as you   (10) know. However, there are* a few hints which you might find   (20)

helpful in taking* typing tests for employment.   (30)

Personnel* and employment offices generally put greater   (40)

stress* on accuracy than on speed. (Remember, while* you are   (50/60)

learning the early emphasis is <u>speed</u>.) On* an employment   (70)

test, aim for accuracy. You are* allowed approximately five   (80)

errors on a five-minute test. No* one expects your typing to   (90)

be perfect on a test.*   (100)

Before you type each letter, say it to yourself.* In   (110)

this way, you can control your fingers.*   (120)

Start off slowly and accurately and you'll* gain speed   (130)

as you go. If you feel yourself make* an error, stop typing   (140)

and then start picking up speed* again. You can avoid making   (150)

one error right* after another this way.   (160)

The first few times* you take an employment test may   (170)

prove discouraging.* Even very experienced, fast typists find   (180)

this* true. But after several interviews and tests, you* will   (190/200)

settle down and do very well. Remember, *most employers expect   (210)

you to be nervous on tests* and allow for this. They will   (220)

also give you two or* three opportunities on the testing.   (230)

Most* important of all--relax! There will always be a*   (240/250)

good number of job opportunities for people who can* type.   (260)

QUESTIONS AND ANSWERS ABOUT TYPING

<u>Shouldn't I type something until it is* perfect?</u>   (10)

    Yes, if you are trying to type a letter* to mail or a   (20)

final report. However, in learning* to type you should never   (30)

type any copy more than* two or three times. After that you   (40)

start practicing your mistakes.* Extensive research has shown   (50)

that people* improve their speed and their accuracy more by*   (60/70)

typing new copy than by typing the same material* over and over (80)

and over again.

<u>I have been typing at* 15 words a minute for a week.   What</u>   (90)

<u>should I do?*</u>   (100)

    In all learning processes you reach plateaus* and this is   (110)

what has happened with your typing. *There are several things   (120)

you can do. First, ignore* all your errors and just push for   (130)

speed. Aim for 18 words a minute on a 1-minute timing and   (140)

then on a* 3-minute timing. Do not count your errors on these* (150/160)

timings. If this doesn't work, try some letters* from another   (170)

section of the typing book. You can* also just use straight copy (180)

to type from. Push* for speed, but don't time yourself. You   (190)

could go* several days without timing yourself and then you*   (200/210)

would see how you had improved.

<u>Why should I waste* time typing letters and reports? Wouldn't</u>   (220)

<u>this* time be better spent trying to improve my speed?*</u>   (230/240)

You are improving your speed and your accuracy* as you type   (250)

the letters and reports. Much research* has been done on   (10)

this and the evidence shows that* your speed actually improves   (20)

more quickly when* typing letters and other production work   (30)

rather than* just straight copy. On your job, the speed that*   (40/50)

is most important is the speed with which you* can type letters   (60)

and reports rather than straight* copy.   (70)

My 1-minute timings are much faster than my* 5-minute timings.   (80)

Why?

        This is very natural and* usual. It is easier to push hard   (90)

for speed in* a short period of time than over a long period   (100)

of* time. Try to maintain your 1-minute pace on a* 5-minute   (120)

timing and you'll find your speed improving.*   (130)

How much progress should I make each day?

        This* will vary from day to day as the learning pattern* is   (150)

irregular. Some days you may improve 2 to 3 or* even 5 words   (160)

a minute. Other days it might be* 1 or 2 words and some days   (170)

you may even go backwards.* However, an average increase is   (180)

1 word per* minute.   (190)

Does age make any difference in learning* to type?   (200)

        A person who is in the habit of attending* school and con-   (210)

centrating on subject matter will* have an easier time learning   (220) to type than someone* who has been away from a desk for a long   (230)

time.* Also students have been used to focusing on the* printed   (240/250)

letter more than a person who has been* keeping house, for example.   (10)

It's this complete* concentration on each letter which will help   (20)

you* improve your typing. Just getting used to sitting* at a   (30/40)

typewriter for 45 minutes can be an adjustment* for people   (50)

who are used to being on their feet* most of the time. A person   (60)

over 30 may find that* it takes slightly longer to gain speed   (70)

in typing* than a high school or college student. An older*   (80/90)

person is in the habit of doing things correctly* the first time   (100)

and may find it difficult to sacrifice* accuracy for speed which   (110)

is very necessary to* do when learning to type.   (120)

Is it very bad to look* at the keyboard?   (130)

    Of course you must look to see* that your fingers are on the   (140)

home-row keys. While* you are typing, you may find you want to   (150)

glance* at the keyboard every so often to reassure yourself.*   (160/170)

Movies of typists of all speeds from very slow* to very fast   (180)

typists at 100 words a minute show* that experienced typists   (190)

do look at the keyboard* more than expected. Another way to   (200)

reassure yourself* is to look at the copy you have typed rather*   (210/220)

than the keyboard. Generally speaking, however,* you will find   (230)

that you can type faster and more* accurately by keeping your   (240)

eyes on the material* you are copying.   (250)

HOW TO MAKE CORRECTIONS

The easiest way to make a correction is to* avoid it   (10)

completely with accurate typing. However,* errors do occur   (20)

and it is important to correct them* so they will not be   (30)

visible.

Various products* are available to help you: special   (40)

typewriter* paper (Corrasable Bond), special typewriter   (50)

erasers,* white-out paper and paint-out liquid, and special* (60/70)

typewriter ribbons. Experiment with the various* products,   (80)

following the directions given by the* manufacturer.   (90)

If you have taken your paper* out of the typewriter   (100)

and discover an incorrect* letter, you should erase it   (110)

carefully or use paint-out* liquid. (It is almost impos-   (120)

sible to use white-out* paper once you have taken your paper   (130)

out of the* typewriter.) Then put your paper back in the*   (140/150)

typewriter and use the paper release to position the* paper   (160)

at the correct print point. Use your variable* linespacer   (170)

on the left-hand cylinder knob to* align your paper vertically. (180)

To practice lining* up your paper at the correct print   (190)

point, follow* these steps now.   (200)

Type the word H A P P Y.* Notice where the bottom of   (210)

the word comes on your* typewriter at your print point   (220)

59

indicator. Just for* practice, use the variable linespacer   (230)

to free roll* your paper down. Now try to get it back in   (240)

position* using the variable linespacer. To check* yourself,   (250/260)

try to type Y on top of the Y in H A P P Y.* Can you do   (270)

it without a shadow?

Now practice* using your paper release to line up   (280)

letters. Notice* where your letters are in relation to the   (290)

print* point indicator on your typewriter. Now move your*   (300/310)

paper by using the paper release and realign your* paper   (320)

to type over the H in H A P P Y. Practice* until you can   (330)

strike over a letter without a* shadow.   (340)

If you make a mistake in the first part* of a letter or   (350)

page, it is usually easiest to* start over. Once past the   (360)

first paragraph, you will* probably find it fastest to correct   (370)

an error.*   (380)

(On a two-page letter, put as little copy as* possible   (390)

on each page. In this way, if you have to* retype a page,   (400)

you won't have as much to retype.)*   (410)

When typing straight copy for practice, do* not <u>stop</u> to   (420)

correct or type over an incorrect letter.* You should be work-   (430)

ing for speed or accuracy.* When you are typing letters,   (440)

however, you will want* to make them mailable. That is with   (450)

<u>no errors* showing</u>.   (460)

CARBONS

Usually everything you type* in an office requires a carbon   (10)

copy. The paper* for the copy is generally a tissue--it takes   (20)

less* room in the files--and does not have the company* letter-   (30/40)

head printed on it.

Insert the carbon* paper between the letterhead and the   (50)

tissue. The* carbon side should go next to the tissue; the* smooth   (60)

side with the printing on it next to the* original.   (70)

When putting the letterhead and carbon* into the typewriter,   (80)

the carbon is facing you.* When you roll the carbon through   (90)

the typewriter,* it gets angry and turns its back on you.   (100)

Sometimes* you may use carbon paper sets with the carbon*   (110/120)

attached to the tissue. When inserting these into* the typewriter,   (130)

make certain the carbon is between* the original and the tissue.   (140)

These pieces of* carbon are thrown away after each use.   (150)

To make* a correction on a carbon copy, erase the incorrect*   (160/170)

letter or use correct-type on the original first,* then erase   (180)

the incorrect letter on the carbon* copy. Now you are ready   (190)

to type the correct letter* on the original.   (200)

Note that a pencil eraser is* often the neatest kind to   (210)

use on the carbon copy.*   (220)

Here are more letters to practice typing. Check position and proofread your work before taking it out of the typewriter.

A two-page letter, memos, call reports, press releases, and résumés are also shown on the following pages. Try typing them for accuracy.

Notice that the comma is *not* underlined in the film title in the following letter. Add the necessary initials at the bottom of the letter:

Date, Mrs. Mary Mansfield, Center for Urban Education, 300

Madison Avenue, New York, NY 10017 Dear Mrs. Mansfield:

Your analysis of our film script outline, <u>A Day in the Death</u>

<u>of Carl</u>, was so constructive I have passed it along to everyone

on our staff.

Although parents and teachers are all agreed on the need to

educate students on the dangers of drug addiction, there seems

to be little agreement on the most effective way of presenting

this information. Indeed, one of the problems is that students

know so much more about drugs than their teachers that teachers

are understandably insecure about dealing with the subject

entirely.

We hope the educational film we are planning will be an acceptable

substitute in these cases, and we are grateful for your invaluable

guidelines. We expect to call upon you again when we have

finished shooting the film in order to get your response to

the footage. Sincerely yours, Gordon Smith, Director of Production.

Date, Mr. Harry Evans, Reading Supervisor, Augusta County

Elementary Schools, Staunton, VA 27701 Dear Mr. Evans: Yes,

those rumors you've heard are correct. We are dropping our

famed Tom and Jane reading system altogether, to be replaced

this spring with a new system of teaching reading that deliberately

avoids any single approach.

The program is too complex to explain in a mere letter, so I

have given your inquiry to our salesman in your territory, who

will invite you to the next conference scheduled for your area,

when a complete demonstration will be given to educators.

For now, let me just explain that our new system consists of

combinations of books, alphabet cards, games and puzzles,

story books and tests.

We are convinced these new methods are necessary because of

the new levels of childhood interest and knowledge, influenced

by television and a more mobile society.

We think you'll agree that with this new reading system,

children will be convinced that reading is fun. Edgar Barnes,

Senior Reading Editor. EB:urs

Date, Miss Mary Rinehart, Ford Placement Agency, 30 Rockefeller

Plaza, New York, NY 10020 Dear Miss Rinehart: This will serve

to commission your agency to begin an immediate search for a

secretary-assistant for one of our top editors. We are assuming

that any candidate you would send us would have more than average
skills, but we are looking for qualities that go beyond accurate
typing and rapid shorthand.

This is basically a trainee spot. The candidate must have a
sound foundation in English grammar, sentence structure,
punctuation and spelling so that she/he can eventually move up
to copy editing on her/his own. This key spot as the assistant
to one of our most important people will give her/him an opportunity
to learn all phases of publishing and is definitely for the
career-motivated candidate.

The salary is open, and the position becomes available next
month. Sincerely, James Peters, Personnel Manager. JP:urs

Check the spelling, paragraph this letter,
and add complimentary closing and initials:

Date, Mrs. Joseph Andrews, 5 Outlook Lane, Mountaintop, MO
54962 Dear Mrs. Andrews, On Friday, April 17, Mrs. Dean Holmes
will ring your doorbell. She is your new Avon Lady and will
be serving you and your naghbors for the coming year. Mrs.
Holmes will be showing you our magnifisent new line of cosmetics.
We have just developped a new perfumed soap and have named
it "Bird of Paradise" because of its exotic fragrence and color.
We know that you will love the luxurious texture of this soap,
Mrs. Andrews, and you will want to use it all the time. John
H. Gringle, Advertising Manager.

64

Dear Mr. Courtland: I am very sorry to learn that you can not

attend the Paper-Work Simplification Clinick in Sacramento.

Yes, judgeing from what I have observed in similar clinics

in San Rafael, Oakland, and Monterey this particuler clinick

focusses direkly on the problems that you face in redusing

expenses for your firm. Should any change of plans inable you

to attend the clinic, Mr. Courtland, please don't hesitate

to call me. I shall ba at the Bradley and I plan to arrie the

Sunday before the clinic. Very truly yours,

Dear Jim: Yes we are exhibiting at the EHA affair in Boston

in December. Because we have found it worth while, not merely

the politic thing to do, we have exhibited with this association

year after year. We recommend your exhibiting. I think a

reunion that weekend with the other Columbia fellows sounds

like a good idea, don't you? Cordially yours,

Date, Mr. Matthew Stockbridge, 100 Elm Street, Troy, NY 12180

Dear Mr. Stockbridge: Your request for a $100 grant to develop

an ecology program for the elementary grade level has been

turned over to me for consideration. Your background in this

area is impressive; it would seem you have the qualifications to make a significant contribution in a field that has excited much concern of late.

The elementary grades would certainly be the most logical and valuable place to begin educating for a lifetime of constructive behavior toward our environment.

Your plan, however, is sketchy in its outline and obscure in its details. We would have to know a great deal more about how you would proceed before we could approve a grant. The enclosed brochure will provide you with guidelines on how your proposal should be submitted.

I shall be pleased to see your revised outline. Sincerely yours, Terrence Jackson, Education Administrator. TJ:urs. Enclosure.

Date, Mr. John Little: I am returning the manuscript you submitted for our appraisal, but because your work did generate some interest among our editors, I wanted to explain just why we are turning it down.

There is a glaring omission in your anthology of American literature in that it doesn't contain a fair, balanced represen-tation of work or writers who are members of non-white minorities. It is now the policy of most publishing houses to attempt to combat racial-ethnic bias by presenting every shade of opinion

and experience; we find this lack of balance in your manuscript
to be its most serious failing.

Perhaps with some changes and additional material, you might
resubmit this anthology, which many of us felt had unusual
merit. Sincerely yours, Charlotte Reed, Senior Editor.

Notice the title Ms., which is applied to women, married and unmarried. Also notice the hyphens in re-examine and in industry-wide:

Date, Ms. Sally Winthrop, Personnel Director, Ace Publishing
Company, 500 Fifth Avenue, New York, NY 10036 Dear Ms. Winthrop:
The time has come for those of us in the communications industry
to re-examine our personnel practices as it becomes more evident
that the financial and status rewards offered by our industry
are no longer sufficient to motivate our employees. Certainly
many young people entering the business world today seem to be
as concerned about fulfilling themselves and utilizing their
skills and abilities as they are about material security.

Because we live in an era of relative prosperity, and a large
proportion of the population need not worry about where the
next meal is coming from, today's employees are looking for
rewards beyond necessities.

We are therefore instituting a series of industry-wide meetings

to discuss these problems. Watch your mail for news of the
location and dates of these important conferences. Sincerely
yours, Jack Reed, Chairman, Personnel Practices Committee.
JR:urs

Notice the carbon copy to Mr. Ambrose:

Date, Mr. Fred B. Grandoe, International Express Club, Ltd.,
131 West 32nd Street, New York, NY 10001 Dear Mr. Grandoe:
My bill arrived this morning, still carrying charges for two
dinners at Charley O's and an airplane ticket to Bermuda.

I have already written you twice (December 3, 19-- and January
6, 19--) explaining that I have never been to Charley O's or
to Bermuda.

These charges are obviously errors and I have no intention of
accepting them. Moreover, it seems to me astonishing that it
should take three months to correct so simple a mistake.

Good public relations would suggest that you take the word of
a long-standing customer, even when it does not agree with
your computer. Computers are not infallible, and neither are
your employees, evidently.

I am sending a copy of this letter to Mr. Ernest Ambrose, your
Vice-President for Customer Relations. I trust that my next
bill will carry the necessary corrections. Sincerely yours,
Franklin P. Smith (Card No. 1/707/693/10) FPS:urs   cc: Mr.
Ernest Ambrose.

The subject line goes *after* the salutation.
Double space after the salutation and after
the subject line. Notice the underscore:

Remember: *Proofread* before taking the
letter out of the typewriter.

Date, Mr. Ernest Stengl, President, Stengl, Werner & Bond,

30 East 42nd Street, New York, NY 10017 Dear Mr. Stengl:

Subject: New Broadhurst Booklet Study of the handsome Widdicomb

line includes several types of furniture that Broadhurst

doesn't make, as I understand it, i.e., kitchen, patio and

game room. I would therefore suggest cutting the number of

pages in the new Broadhurst booklet to half, or 16.

As I see it, that would allow a double spread for each furniture

grouping, with ample space below the photographs for description

of the individual pieces. Since the color pix you now have

do not include the new designs, we should get together and

make arrangements to complete the set. Finding a studio that

can accept large pieces and hold them for any length of time

is always something of a problem.

Of course, our organization can plan with you to prop the sets,

supervise the background construction and arrange for the

flowers, as we have in the past. Do let me know if you agree

about the size of the booklet. If expense is no problem, we

can probably stretch to fill the full 32 pages. Cordially,

Barbara McNair, Vice-President. BMcN:urs

Skip a line after the city and state for the attention line. Double space between the attention line and salutation. Notice the underscore:

Date, Ace Publishing Company, 437 Madison Avenue, New York,

NY 10022 Attention: <u>Harlow Mitchell, Director of Sales</u>

Gentlemen: We have just contracted to publish a series of

12 posters by the widely-known artist and designer, Milton

Kane. These should be ready for distribution late in the

year and will also be produced as a hardcover book.

The posters will be topical, in the tradition for which Mr.

Kane is already justly famous. You will recall his "Earth

Day" and "California Grape" posters of last year.

Is your firm interested in negotiating for the distribution

rights of these posters and the book? There is a large market

for these handsome graphics; we wanted to give you first

crack at distributing them because of the outstanding job

you did with our celebrity posters last year.

The grapevine has already gotten word of this, and we've

received interest from other distributors, so we'd appreciate

your quick decision. Sincerely yours, James Aldridge,

Managing Editor. JA:urs

FOUNDATION OF MODERN DANCE

630 Third Avenue
New York, NY 10017

December 8, 19--

Ms. Joan Kimberly
The Rich Foundation
320 East 43rd Street
New York, NY 10017

Dear Ms. Kimberly:

As secretary of the Foundation of Modern Dance, I am writing
to you on behalf of the James Abalanthe Dance Company. The
time has come, Ms. Kimberly, for the Rich Foundation to recognize
the vital importance of modern dance to our cultural heritage.

Modern dance has been recognized by the United States Government
as one of the three integral art forms of America. The other
two are the Broadway musical and jazz as developed from the
Negro spiritual. If the government has finally voiced its
belief in these three important contributions to American
culture, is it not time for the wealthy foundations to do so,
too?

There has been a definite lack of monetary support for the
modern dance in the 50-odd years that it has been developing.
Patronage has come from a select few. As dance is becoming
an accepted part of American culture, do you not feel that a
foundation, such as Rich, which is interested in the advancement
of the United States in the fields of education, public affairs,
science and engineering, could not include modern dance in its
widening scope?

The name of Martha Graham is synonymous with modern dance
around the world. She has broken the way for the many companies
that have followed. However, the new people in dance must
be recognized. James Abalanthe is the person who could bring
modern dance on to the level of a pure art form again.

To get beyond the technique instilled by the "Grahamesque" school
of dance, he broke with Miss Graham. He does not lean toward the
professionalism of a Merce Cunningham. He has found the beauty
of pure movement. The poetry of free movement which he portrays
on stage is the most vital step in modern dance.

Now, Ms. Kimberly, the steps to follow must come from a foundation
desirous to promote the general cultural heritage of our country.
The Foundation of Modern Dance, which has been formed for the
James Abalanthe Dance Company, is appealing to the Rich Foundation
to see the necessity of backing modern dance.

Money granted to the James Abalanthe Dance company would be
divided wisely to serve various needs. These include:

1. The expansion of the present studio to
    enable more students to have the oppor-
    tunity to study under James Abalanthe.

2. The commission of new dances to be performed
    on tour.

3. The payment of salary to the manager
    who is required for the booking of the
    tours and the general handling of the
    company's business.

4. The weekly salaries of the dancers when on
    tour with the company.

I hope that you, as head of all grants in the art field, will
find it worthy of your attention to pursue a grant for the James
Abalanthe Dance Company. Please contact me if you have any questions
which I could answer. Perhaps we could arrange to meet for lunch
one day next week to discuss the application for a grant.

Sincerely,

FOUNDATION OF MODERN DANCE

Kelly Holt, Secretary

KH:jm
Enclosures

MEMORANDUMS: Letters are sent to persons outside your organization. A memo is sent to a person inside the organization.

Many companies have their own preprinted memo forms. However, you may type your own form. Here are two good examples. Try typing them.

June 19, 19--

To: George Gordon

From: James E. Spofford

Subject: Gourmet Food Packages

Last night my wife came up with what may turn out to be a great idea.

We had a few friends in for cocktails and she remarked that it was a "pain in the neck" to prepare unusual hors d'oeuvres because of the necessity of going to so many different shops to get these items.

"Why doesn't someone invent a handy package that contains several of these foods?" she said.

It occurred to me, later, that there just might be a market for something like that.

Why not kick the idea around with the boys in Marketing and Research? Let me know what you think of the idea.

J. E. S.

JES:urs

MEMORANDUM

TO: Gloria Burns   June 19, 19--

FROM: Thomas Nichols, Creative Director

SUBJECT: Advertising Industry Awards

This is to congratulate you for participating in and being
named a winner in the annual Advertising Industry Award
Festival for copy writing and display ads. By winning
one of these most coveted awards for our agency, you
have added considerably to our growing reputation as
being one of the most creative new agencies in the business.

We know that your personal sense of pride has been
sufficiently rewarded through this honor, but as an
agency we wanted to acknowledge our own pride in the
talent we breed. Therefore, we are running a house
ad in the next issue of Advertising Age, containing
photographs of the prize winners and their award-
winning ads.

Keep up the fine work.

TN:urs

CALL REPORT

Client: BABCO MANUFACTURING COMPANY

Contact: Robert C. Murphy

Date: June 19, 19--

On the above date, I met with Mr. Francis Ambrose in Chicago.
The following decisions were made:

1. We will run our forthcoming ad campaign as originally
    specified. The agency proposals for schedule, copy
    theme and layout were approved, with corrections as
    indicated on the copy.

2. We have already cancelled an insertion in Baking
    Industry in July. The client is considering cancelling
    Bakers' Weekly. It was pointed out to Mr. Ambrose
    that cutting the page in Bakers' Weekly puts the
    schedule below the frequency rate originally contracted
    for. This could possibly affect their rate charges
    for all ads as well as those of the Container Division.
    Mr. Ambrose will discuss this further with Mr. Mosbach
    and let us know his decision.

3. We will write Baking Industry and Bakers' Weekly to
    request utmost care in handling the reproduction of
    Babco's ads. Mr. Ambrose agreed that it was not our
    red plate but their printing that put the last ad
    out of register.

Mr. Ambrose now has the cost estimates for the container ads,
the reprints of those ads and one covering the cost of a black-
and-white plate. He will sign the originals and return them
to us as soon as the ads are approved.

cc: Mr. Francis Ambrose
     Mr. John Morris

Distribution: AAE, DT, CM, BK, PW, LP, EH

PRESS RELEASE

Reidman & Welsh, Inc. *Public Relations Department *
         * 630 Park Avenue * New York, NY 10021 *
                (212) Locust 5-6800

From: Frieda Baltzer   For: Slim-Line Foods, Inc.

                FOR RELEASE AFTER 2:20 p.m.

                FRIDAY, SEPTEMBER 13, 19--

NEW SLIM-LINE LOW SUGAR LINE FOR CALORIE-COUNTING CONSUMERS

SAN FRANCISCO, CA, September 12. Slim-Line's canned fruits
go back to nature with the new line of calorie-reduced
products. These new non-cyclamate fruits have no artificial
sweeteners, and their new low-sugar formulation approximates
the natural flavor and sugar level of fresh fruit.

        The new cans with their bright green label go into
national distribution this month with a full assortment of
fruits and juices. The calorie count for most is comparable
to fresh fruits, and far lower than regular canned fruits.
Calorie comparisons on the labels compare Slim-Line with
regular canned fruits; for instance, a half-cup portion of
Slim-Line apricots contains 56 calories, while a similar
portion of regular canned fruit contains 110.

        For people on special diets, Slim-Line labels also contain
a carbohydrate and sugar content analysis and comparison.

        Slim-Line canned fruits are priced in line with regular
canned fruits. The new line is expected to sell on regular
grocery shelves, rather than diet sections. Samples will
be coming to you under separate cover.

How to Type Tables, Lists, and Charts

Material in tabular form, numbers and words can be typed quickly and clearly by using the following procedure.

First type the longest line in the first column, then type six periods for the six spaces you want to allow between columns, then type the longest line in the last column. As an example, for the Sneeze on Monday table, you would type:

Sneeze on Wednesday......Sneeze for sorrow

Center this line on your page according to the instructions in Step 7 and set your left margin. (Go to the center of your page and backspace once for every two letters and spaces.) Then tap out on your space bar *Sneeze on Wednesday . . . . . .* and set your tab for the second column. Now you are ready to type the following Mother Goose rhyme. Center it on your page according to the instructions already given, or by the backspace method following the step-by-step directions given after it.

Sneeze on Monday

Sneeze on Monday	Sneeze for danger
Sneeze on Tuesday	Kiss a stranger
Sneeze on Wednesday	Get a letter
Sneeze on Thursday	Something better
Sneeze on Friday	Sneeze for sorrow
Sneeze on Saturday	Joy tomorrow

1. Clear all tab stops on your typewriter following the instructions.

2. Center the title according to the instructions and underscore.

3. Skip 3 lines.

4. Check the largest number of letters and spaces in each column.

5. Go to the center of your page and backspace:

    a. One time for every 2 letters and spaces in the longest line of column 1. (A total of 19 letters and spaces, so you backspace 9 times.

    b. One time for every 2 spaces between columns. The *customary number of spaces is 6,* so you backspace 3 times.

    c. One time for every 2 letters and spaces in the longest line of column 2.

    d. Set your left margin at this spot.

6. You have 2 columns, so you will want to set a tab stop at the beginning of the second column. (Your left margin acts as the edge of your first column.) To find the tab stop point for the second column (it probably will not be at the exact center of the page) from your left margin, tap the space bar one time for each letter and space for the longest line of column 1 and once for each of the 6 spaces between the columns. Press the tab set.

7. Now you are ready to type the table on sneezes. Try it.

Does your table look like the one above? Are the margins on both sides even? If not, check to see if the center of your paper is at the center mark on your typewriter. If you had trouble with this, try it over again, following the directions step by step.

Another way of centering which some people prefer is to count the total number of letters and spaces in the title and divide by

2. Drop the final letter if the number is uneven. Then, from the center of your page, backspace the number which results from dividing the total letters and spaces by 2.

You can also set up a table using this method:

1. Count the number of letters and spaces in the longest line of column 1.

2. Add the spaces between the columns, 6.

3. Add the number of letters and spaces in the longest line of column 2.

4. Add these numbers together and divide by 2.

5. Go to the center of your space and backspace the number of times indicated in Step 4. Your left margin should be at that point.

6. Follow the instructions given in the preceding section starting with 6.

Try centering this chart as you did the Mother Goose Rhyme:

TYPING GOALS

High school students who type	25 words a minute
People who learn for their personal use	30 words a minute
College students who type	30-35 words a minute
Clerk-typists	40-45 words a minute
Receptionists	40-45 words a minute
Beginning secretaries	50-55 words a minute
Writers who type	55 words a minute
Reporters	60 words a minute
Legal or executive secretaries	65 words a minute

Résumé for a person with
limited experience:

NANCY A. JOBHUNTER

144 East 44th Street
New York, NY 10017
212/867-7667

EDUCATION

New York University. B.A. degree, June 19--. Honors
in English.

Radcliffe College. 19--. Publishing Procedures Course.
The University of Chicago. 19-- - 19--
Betty Owen Secretarial Systems, Inc. 19--.
(Typing and shorthand.)

HONORS AND EXTRA CURRICULAR ACTIVITIES

New York University: Dean's List, Coat of Arms Honorary
Society, Founder's Day Honarary Award, Sigma Delta Omicron
(English Honorary Society). Editor, Washington Square Review.
Member of the Chorus.

The University of Chicago: Mortar Board; Student Politics;
Business Manager, Yearbook.

VOCATIONAL EXPERIENCE

19--   Friends of the Park, Secretarial Work.

19--   New York University Hospital, New York City, Nurse's Aide.

19--   The Cleveland Press, Cleveland, Ohio, Copygirl.

19--   Camp Robinson Crusoe, Sturbridge, Massachusetts, Counselor.

SKILLS AND FOREIGN LANGUAGES

Shorthand 100 words per minute.
Typing 60 words per minute.
Fluent Spanish. Reading knowledge of French and Italian.

Résumé for an experienced
person:

ANNE HOWARD

235 West 23rd Street
New York, NY 10011
OR 4-7340

BUSINESS EXPERIENCE

19-- to   EXECUTIVE SECRETARY
present   Columbia Artists Management
                 New York, New York

        In addition to the regular secretarial duties,
I am responsible for the supervision and training of
the secretaries and clerks in the lecture division.
Administrative duties include scheduling and travel
arrangements for approximately 100 lecturers.

19-- to   SECRETARY
19--   Ted Bates Advertising Agency
                 New York, New York

        Diversified duties in the radio-TV department.
Talent payment records, contracts and liason with the
studio. Beginning job after graduation from high
school.

Summers   CLERK
19-- and   Young Audiences, Inc.
19--   Boston, Massachusetts

        Clerical work in small research firm.

EDUCATION

        Robert E. Lee High School. Ithaca, New York.
        Graduated 19--.

        Betty Owen Secretarial Systems. New York.
        Typing and Shorthand. Summer 19--.

SKILLS AND FOREIGN LANGUAGES

        Shorthand 100 words per minute.
        Typing 60 words per minute.
        Fluent Spanish. Reading knowledge of French and Italian.